Natural Medicine from the Kitchen

A Treasure Trove of Traditional Gastronomic Remedies

Thomas E. Duckworth
Doctor of Kototama Life Medicine

Natural Medicine from the Kitchen

1972 – 2017

This book is dedicated to the principle that an informed citizenry is necessary for a healthy society.

This information comes to us through our ancestors; would we copyright it to keep it from our children?

Compiled by Thomas E. Duckworth, L.Ac.
In New Mexico and Missouri
and a few other places
Doctor of Kototama Life Medicine
Executive Director
Institute of American Acupuncture and Life Medicine, Inc.
Saint Louis, Missouri

Dedication

Masahilo M. Nakazono O-sensei
Founder: Kototama Life Medicine
Physician, Priest, Warrior, Humanist

In the summer of 1980, O-Sensei queried, "Do you want to learn?" "Yes, Sensei," I answered. "Good," he replied. "To learn, you must teach." In September of that year, he sat me down in front of a classroom of students and I began sharing.

This book and much of what I share is due to the knowledge, wisdom, love and challenge that Masahilo M. Nakazono O-sensei imparted.

Introduction

I devoted over ten complete uninterrupted years immersed in the study of Kototama Life Medicine under the guidance of its founder/creator, Masahilo M. Nakazono.

My studies with Masahilo M. Nakazono also included Spiritual explorations, Japanese Folk Medicine, Martial Arts, First Aid and Trauma Care, Macrobiotic Diet practices and trout fishing (sitting quietly). I was shown how to make and use albi plasters, how to filet crappie for sushi, how to make miso, how to make Umeboshi plums, how to make ginger soaks, how to eat, how to sit quietly, how to generate warmth and how to enhance Ki.

I read in an old cookbook, "Man digs his grave with his teeth." Our digestive system is complex and quite nicely self-evolved. The first organs of the digestive system are the teeth, 32 very specific types of teeth that provide very specific action: broad flat grinding teeth, not unlike horses' teeth, for breaking and grinding seeds, nuts and grasses; teeth that shred and chew, similar to the teeth of goats, camels, and other vegetarians; four "canines," useful for tearing muscle meat. The teeth know what to eat. The digestion system knows how to function. GOD isn't stupid. Chewing triggers the excretion of digestive enzymes from glands in the mouth, the chemistry necessary for the digestion of starches. When food is swallowed without being chewed or bites of food are washed down with liquids, vital ingredients and processes of the digestive system are by-passed or diluted; this paves the road to future digestive issues. Pay attention to your DNA, your heritage; what were YOUR ancestors chewing on? Devitalized and denatured foods, no matter how 'good' they taste, lack essential elements that keep the body supplemented with the vitamins and minerals needed to replace those being consumed in the normal body process of living. If these necessary nutritional elements are supplied to the body, old age comes on gently and almost unnoticed.

Can these nutrients be gained through pills and supplements? No, but maybe if you chew the pill/supplement very slowly.

The brain's willingness to mistreat the body is still under investigation.

What else? Leave the table with your stomach a quarter full of fluids, half full of solids, a quarter empty. Exercise: Walking; pushing the plate away.

I am putting this information together for my children, my students, my friends and those who are "taking care of business." This is part of my attempt to pay back for all that I have gained, to help heal all the wounds I have helped create. If you are interested in healing, helping, caring, this book might prove interesting, informative, helpful, perhaps even necessary. Be well.

We are never too old to become younger; never too old to have a childhood.

Thomas E. Duckworth
drtduck42@sbcglobal.net

Table of Contents

FOOD AS MEDICINE and THERAPEUTIC USAGES: COMPRESSES, PLASTERS AND SOAKS *1*

TREATMENT BY SYMPTOMS 71

FOOD AS MEDICINE

The body creates every cell from the nutrients ingested by that body. You will create more cells of your body from the time of conception to six months after your birth than you will from birth to age 90. Obviously, what your mother was eating during your embryonic development is as important as what you are eating right now. And your children?

THERAPEUTIC USAGES: COMPRESSES, PLASTERS AND SOAKS

When a plaster is applied, pain, pressure or other strange sensations may be experienced. This may be regarded as a good sign. It probably means that the plaster is doing its job; the waste is breaking up and will soon appear on the surface of the skin. If I am wrong, I apologize.

(Once I suggested to a neighbor who had twisted his ankle to apply an albi plaster that I provided; he did so. A few hours later, he called because he felt the albi was trying to pull out the screws in his surgically repaired earlier injury. I suggested he stop using the plaster. Pay attention to sensations, but they are probably part of the healing process.)

ALBI PLASTER

The main ingredient in an albi plaster is taro, a root vegetable that looks somewhat like a potato. In America, it is known as "taro"; Puerto Ricans call it or iya otiya. Taro is also used as food. When purchasing taro, choose those roots that are small, young, fresh, and light in color (like a white potato). It is advisable to peel off the brown outside skin.

The albi plaster is used for various complaints and can be applied to various parts of the body, both front and back; over the eye (for eye trouble), behind the ear (for ear trouble), on the face, throat and legs – everywhere.

The appropriate mixture for an albi plaster varies, depending on the water content of the taro.

One mixture contains 50 percent grated taro, 5 percent grated ginger and 45 percent flour (white flour is best for plasters because it is the most glutinous). Use this combination whenever a higher consistency is desired.

Another mixture might have the following composition: 70 percent taro, 20 percent flour, 10 percent ginger.

Slowly add just enough water to this taro, flour, ginger mix to make a thick dough, like bread or pie dough. Application thickness should be between ¼ and ½ inch.

Use cotton gauze to hold the albi mixture over the affected area. With the initial application, change the plaster after two hours. Then change every eight to twelve hours. It is best to keep it on day and night. Change at least every twelve hours.

Should the plaster cause a skin irritation, apply sesame oil to the inflamed area.

ADZUKI BEANS

Adzuki Beans are small red beans used commonly in Japan, known for their rich quality as food and medicine. Beans cook best in a pressure cooker or heavy clay pot. The beans and juice from the beans can both be used as medicine.

USES

For kidney trouble and symptoms related to kidney issues – such as edema, swelling, gout, puffiness or urinary tract issues, eat only adzuki beans, nothing else, for two or three days. This is often quite effective.

For prolonged menstruation, try eating five raw adzuki beans, being careful to chew them well. This is effective in terminating the bleeding.

A half cup of adzuki bean juice taken at least half an hour before meals for two days is excellent for most kidney complaints. If kept in the refrigerator to prevent spoiling, heat the juice before consuming.

PREPARATION

Beans

Rinse the beans in a strainer. Combine one cup of beans and two and a half cups of cold water in a pot. If you are using a pressure cooker, bring up the pressure, lower the flame, and allow the beans to cook for one hour. Remove pressure cooker from the stove and hold under running water to bring down the pressure. Then open and add a small amount of water and the necessary salt; two and a half cups of water and a half teaspoon of salt is quite sufficient. Cook uncovered for ten minutes or so. The beans are now ready to eat.

If you wish to cook the beans in a heavy pot you may do so, but in this case, you must add more water, a half cup perhaps. You can start cooking the beans over the stove. When they begin to boil, put them in a hot oven for two hours or so.

Juice

Combine one cup of beans and five cups of water. Boil the beans for one hour, then remove the juice. (You may continue cooking the beans, of course.) A half-cup of adzuki juice taken at least a half an hour before meals for two days is excellent for most kidney complaints. If it is kept in the refrigerator to prevent spoiling (good idea!), the juice should be heated before consumption.

BLACK BEANS

Black beans, popular in Latin America food and in use throughout the world, are good sources of fiber, protein and iron.

USES

As medicine, the beans can be used for insensitivity during sexual activity or loss of libido. Black Bean juice is very effective for treating hoarseness and laryngitis. Black Bean juice taken over a prolonged period (two to three months) helps regulate irregular, inconsistent menstruation. Drink a half cup three times a day.

PREPARATION

Black beans and black bean juice should be prepared in the same manner as adzuki beans and adzuki bean juice.

For insensitivity during sexual activity or loss of libido, steam one cup of black beans until soft, then dry them, taking whatever time is necessary; add a half cup of black sesame seeds and grind the mixture into a powder. Take 1 spoon mixed with hot water three times a day before meals.

BUCKWHEAT, Cream of

USES

Buckwheat is exceptional for achieving energy and warmth. It strengthens the kidneys. It is an excellent breakfast cereal for the entire family during the winter. It is a mountain food. What does that mean? It is all for your studies; carry on.

PREPARATION

There are two ways to make cream of buckwheat: with buckwheat flour or with toasted buckwheat grouts ground in an electric blender or flour mill.

Use one cup of flour and one teaspoon of corn oil. Heat the oil, taking care not to burn it. Keeping the heat low, add the flour, stir constantly and rapidly with a wooden spoon so that the flour does not burn. After five minutes, the color of the flour should be light brown and evenly colored. Set aside to cool. Put the cooled flour in a pan with four cups of water. Place over a high heat, continuing to stir until mixture reaches its boiling point. Lower the heat considerably. Keep covered while cooking.

Grind grouts in a blender and use the same procedure as above. Use one cup of buckwheat grouts and four cups of water. Add salt to taste.

BURDOCK ROOT

Burdock as a root vegetable is an ingredient in many recipes for soups and stews. It is a natural digestive aid, intestinal cleanser and powerful medicine for intestinal inflammations. It cools and purifies the blood. It eliminates toxins and helps control cell mutation. It is known in Japan and China for treating appendicitis.

USES

My daughter was seven when she experienced severe lower right quadrant pain. The medical doctor said she thought it might be appendicitis and recommended "exploratory surgery." I called Sensei; he suggested a shot glass full of burdock juice and to wait twenty minutes to see what happens. I did that, called him back, and told him nothing had happened. "Good," said Sensei, "that means it is not appendicitis. Bring her to me."

Abdominal handwork that encouraged bowel activity and a stern grandfatherly lecture about chewing food properly saved her from a very unnecessary surgical procedure. It is now 40 years later and she still has all her organs.

PREPARATION

You can chew the root but a juicer will provide a concentrate dose, about one and a half ounces per dose. As a natural digestive aid, intestinal cleanser and powerful medicine for intestinal inflammations, drink three to four doses per day for one day beyond the last signs of any symptoms.

For infections, boils and abscesses, use the crushed roots and leaves of Burdock as a poultice. Change every four to six hours.

CARP SOUP

Throughout history, the carp has been one of the most valued freshwater fish. It was, at times, only for royalty; in other times, it was proposed as a food for the whole world. The carp is one of the most widely eaten freshwater fish all over the planet and one of the most valued, except in North America, where it is considered "trash fish" and gets no respect. It is thought to be unhealthy and said to be nasty tasting and difficult to prepare.

People who eat carp know this poor reputation is unwarranted. Few fish are palatable when caught in foul water. Carp don't taste very good if they are caught in polluted waters; caught in unpolluted lakes or rivers, they are quite edible. During preparation, take care to remove all the blood, glands, mud vein and dark meat; this will minimize any muddy taste.

USES

Carp soup is very beneficial for those of us in delicate health; it is especially recommended for tuberculosis, anemia, arthritis, rheumatism and cancer. This is an excellent nourishing soup in post-partum care. It will assist in post-partum bleeding, cramping, uterine contractions and delivery of the placenta, as well as stimulate lactation.

PREPARATION

· 4 pounds' carp (small-scale carp)
· 1 dozen burdock roots
· 3 heaping tablespoons of miso
· 2 tablespoons of sesame oil
· 1-2 cups used bancha tea leaves

Fresh carp is best. If possible, remove only the guts and the gallbladder. Cut the fish into half-inch slices, using everything – head, fins, scales. Shred the burdock root into shavings.

Sauté these shavings in sesame oil for twenty minutes over a slow flame. Place the slices of fish over the burdock, adding enough water to cover. It is best to cook carp in a heavy pot.

Now tie the bancha leaves in a cheesecloth and place over the fish. Cover, bring to boil, and simmer until the bones become soft enough to eat (six to eight hours). Now add miso paste previously diluted in a small amount of warm water and let the soup simmer another hour.

You can eat everything in the soup – bones, scales, fins, head – everything should melt in your mouth. The soup has a strong but excellent taste.

CARP PLASTER

Carp plaster on the chest, upper back, or both is an effective treatment for pneumonia.

Buy a whole carp from a fish market. Make an incision in the throat from eye to eye. Drain one tablespoon of blood from the incision and have the patient drink this.

Next remove the organs and discard them. Then chop the meat into small pieces. Spread the chopped meat on the patient's chest.

Keep a constant check on the body temperature. When it reaches 98.6, remove the plaster.

If carp is not available, horse meat might be substituted; however, beef is not effective.

CHLOROPHYLL PLASTER

This plaster serves as a substitute for the albi plaster when albi is not available. It is a very easy plaster to prepare. When you become an expert, you will be able to wander the fields and select the best-suited greens. Until then, here is a simple preparation that does not require much expertise. Use fresh green plant leaves. Radish tops, for example, are very good; the same goes for carrot tops, Swiss chard, watercress, parsley, spinach, etc. Many wild grasses are also suitable. Vegetables such as purple cabbage, white cabbage and lettuce are not so green.

With a knife, fine chop the greens or chop greens in a blender or food processor, to create a well-blended mixture. This is 70 percent of the ingredients. Add 25 percent flour and 5 percent grated ginger. Add enough water to make a thick paste.

Apply to affected area. Change in two hours and every four to six hours thereafter.

Apply a fresh plaster before going to bed.

CORN SILK TEA

The dried or fresh tassels of the corn plant; fresh is preferred.

USES

Drink half a cup of corn silk tea three times a day a half hour before meals as an excellent remedy for kidney stones, bladder issues, incontinence, any urinary discomfort and high blood pressure.

PREPARATION

Dry some corn silk. Add 20 grams (about one handful) to three cups of water and boil until the liquid is reduced by half. Let cool, strain and drink. May sweeten with local honey.

or

One tablespoonful of chopped corn silk to a cup of near-boiling water; cover and steep about twenty minutes; until cool enough to drink. Strain and drink. May be sweeten with local honey.

DAIKON RADISH DRINK

There are several types of radishes available in the market, the most common is the Cherry Belle radish but Daikon radish is the most popular from the medicinal point of view. Another radish popular for its healing properties is the black radish, common in the West. Daikon (Jap: dai- great/large, kon-root) radish is common in the East. It is also known as Winter Radish, Japanese Radish and Chinese Radish. Do not peel or remove the skin.

USE

For colds; induces sweating, encourages a fever and aids in gall bladder issues. Digestant. Raw, grated, it aids digestion of fats in a meal. Cooked daikon aids elimination of stored fats. All radishes stimulate bile production and help break down fats; the black radish is especially excellent for your gallbladder.

PREPARATION

Recipe 1:

Add one tablespoon of grated daikon radish to one cup boiling water, steep ten minutes. Drink hot. Wrap up in blankets in bed. One cup every other day.

Recipe 2:

· 3 tablespoons grated radish
· ½ teaspoon grated ginger
· 1 teaspoon soy sauce
· 1 pint of boiling water or bancha tea

Boil water/bancha tea and add ingredients. Reduce heat and let simmer for a few minutes. Do not squeeze the grated radish. It is better to use the entire radish, not just the juice, so that the mixture will remain longer in the stomach. If only the liquid is used, the drink will pass through the body too quickly. This drink is good for causing sweating and breaking fever. It is also beneficial for liver trouble, since one of the functions of the liver is to adjust body temperature.

Recipe 3:

· 1 cup of juice from grated radish
· 1 cup of water

This version of the radish drink is used generally for inducing urination. Corn silk tea, pickled apples, and watermelon are also effective for this condition.

This recipe may be very powerful at the early onset of 'flu'. If there is a low-grade fever or the very beginning onset of a fever, ingest Recipe # 2, cover with blankets and sweat the fever out. This will result in a cure (probably).

EGG OIL

Egg oil is a traditional Naturopathic medicine of Japan that has regained usage and popularity in recent times. It is made commercially in Japan and the recipe has come to us through Naboru Muramoto, Macrobiotic teacher and author of "Healing Ourselves." I was introduced to the medical use and practical methods of production of egg oil by my beloved and esteemed teacher, Dr. M. Masahilo Nakazono Osensei.

Egg oil preparation is mechanical. The more often you do it, the easier and more productive it becomes. Egg oil is extracted by cooking the yolks of fertile eggs until they turn into a carbon mush and exude oil. It has been used for centuries as a topical hair and skin treatment, as well as in medicine. It is directly applied for dandruff, acne, dryness, hair loss, premature greying of hair and "aging skin."

USES

Egg oil is an excellent treatment for vascular insufficiency or dysfunction, including CVA (stroke), hypertension, arteriosclerosis. It may breakdown HDL cholesterol. Its effects on the circulatory system influences such symptoms as lethargy, inability to get motivated in the morning, heaviness of head, tight neck and shoulders, mild headaches, sporadic low back pain.

Hemorrhoids are treated by direct application. It has also been credited with sexual rejuvenation.

Dosage: three to nine drops, two to three times a day, at or after meal. One respected teacher recommended a half teaspoon (thirty drops) twice a day.

It is my respectful opinion that smaller dosages are quite beneficial for all, while larger dosages may be too much of a shock for some.

PREPARATION

For a small amount, use four to six eggs. Depending on the eggs and technique, twelve eggs should yield one to two ounces of oil. Separate the yolk and the egg white. Use only the yolk. Scramble and slow cook the yolks in a cast iron skillet, pottery cooking pan or copper lined stainless frying pan until they begin to burn, showing brown instead of yellow. Reduce the heat a bit and continue cooking and stirring. As the eggs "burn up," they blacken (carbonizing), continue stirring constantly. At this stage, oil visually emerges from the tar-like mess that was once egg yoks. Tilt the pan to get the oil to collect and pool free of debris. It can further be strained or filtered. Store the oil in an amber bottle. It will keep for months. You can store it refrigerated for up to three years; at room temperature for a year. If handled carefully, it remains sterile for up to five years.

Contraindications: Take a drop or two, if heart palpitations or tachycardia begin soon after, quit taking it. If higher dosages produce these signs, exercise caution; if continuing use, keep it at 1-3 drops twice a week. People with egg allergies to eggs have taken egg oil without incident. Caution is noted and advised.

Possible Side Effects: Heart palpitations, stop taking the oil.

Patches of dry, itchy skin may appear weeks after starting the ingestion of egg oil. If so, stop oil until it clears up, then continue with a smaller dose.

Further reference: http://m.wikihow.com/Make-Egg-Oil-at-Home

EGGPLANT

Eggplant is a species of nightshade grown for its edible fruit. Used in dishes from Italy to Asia. In recipes, it is used as a substitute for meat.

Traditionally, the leaves and roots are juiced or boiled to make a tonic for throat and stomach troubles, asthma, skin diseases, rheumatism, inflammation, intestinal hemorrhages, foot pain, coughs, anorexia, toothache, or as a general stimulant.

USES

The obvious cluster of warts on the back of my 12-year-old son's hand was a social embarrassment. He wanted them gone! We tried a few herbal folk remedies and consulted with the medical profession. They were willing to freeze, cut or chemo the warts but offered no guarantees.

Sensei told my son that he had to eliminate red meat and sugar from his diet and to keep raw eggplant taped to the warts. He followed instructions. The warts were gone in about a week. He returned to meat eating, the warts did not return.

I have recommended this approach multiple times. The acidity of sugar and red meat creates the correct environment for this virus to thrive in, although, of those two sources, sugar seems to be worse.

Eggplants made into miso pickles are effective against gout. When included occasionally in one's diet, eggplant can prove very beneficial for certain expansive (Yang) conditions, especially for an excessive inflammation causing dysfunction of the kidney system or excessiveness in the "Three Heat Centers" (San Sho) of Traditional Oriental Anatomy.

Eggplant, prepared as a meal with a variety of recipes, also has the advantage of satisfying a craving for expansive food.

The satisfaction it provides can help the diner escape the nagging desire for many kinds of food.

PREPARATION

For warts, slice a thick, half to three-quarter inch, piece of the eggplant flesh, not the skin, and place on warts with tape or band aid. Change the eggplant/bandage as needed but at least every eight hours.

One recommended method of preparation for meals is to slice the eggplant thinly and sprinkle with salt. Let it sit awhile. Then, quick fry the eggplant in oil and then continue cooking in a small amount of water. There are eggplant recipes everywhere.

GIN-SOAKED RAISINS

This recipe came to me from Hugh Morris, a delightful and knowledgeable fellow who swore this is all he needed for his arthritic discomforts. I recommend trying it for any joint pain.

PREPARATION

Start with golden raisins. Put them in a shallow bowl, pour in enough gin to barely cover them. Let stand uncovered until the gin is almost completely evaporated. Depending on the environment, this could take a few days to a week or more. If dust is a factor, you can cover with a towel or cheesecloth. When they are ready and still moist; store in a tight container. Refrigeration not needed.

Eat nine raisins a day until pain is gone. Relief may be rapid.

GINGER

Ginger root, or simply ginger, is widely used as a spice and medicine. It is high in the vitamins niacin (B3) and B3 and the minerals iron and manganese. It can be eaten raw, reduced to a juice or an oil, or used topically as a poultice or a soak.

USES

From backaches to bone spurs, headaches to hemorrhoids, the use of ginger is continually being researched and more uses of its healing powers keep being discovered.

In Far Eastern Medicine, we use ginger root to stimulate the organs, provide heat and restore Ki, Vital Force. Ki, the Life Energy of the Universe, animates all life. Stagnation of Ki impairs function and results in disease.

Sore throat, swollen glands, sleeplessness, mental disturbance, unexpected or unexplained pain anywhere in the body, nervous system and circulation problems are just some of the manifestations of Ki disharmony. Use ginger in treating dysfunctions attributable to Ki stagnation.

Ginger is quite useful for digestive problems, such as nausea, colitis, diverticulosis, indigestion, diarrhea, anorexia, morning sickness and motion sickness. Reports from the British medical journal, Lancet, indicate that capsules of powdered ginger root are twice as effective as Dramamine for coping with motion sickness. The dosage prescribed was two capsules (940 milligrams) of powdered ginger. The ginger should be taken in capsules to avoid gastro-intestinal irritation, which can be severe.

This form of ginger ingestion is helpful with vomiting and diarrhea of gastro-intestinal flu. Each person is different and some may need more than others. Some folk have needed as much as ten to twelve capsules an hour. Take care not to irritate the upper digestive tract.

Ginger is also useful for menstrual cramps, hot flashes, muscular spasms and circulation problems. Eating a piece of fresh raw ginger about the size of your thumb may help the pain and bleeding of hemorrhoids.

Externally, it addresses joint problems including arthritis, gout, bursitis, curvature of the spine, muscle contractions, bone spurs, pain relief, inflammation, headache, earache, dandruff, skin problems and bronchitis. Clearly, ginger belongs in the medicine cabinet as well as the kitchen.

Note: If you have a heart condition, please consult with a Meridian Therapist or a knowledgeable ginger user or physician before soaking in a ginger bath.

Ginger Bath

Ginger can be used as a soak or in the bath to promote circulation, address bone spurs, and ease arthritic pain and trauma. Use as a soak by pouring a ginger compress solution into a container appropriate for the hand/wrist, foot/ankle, or elbow. Soak until the solution cools down or the skin holds an intense color. The mixture can be reheated twice.

For a bath, the preparation is the same as for the ginger compress except that, because it is a larger volume of water, it requires more ginger. For a shallow bathtub, use one and half to two pounds of grated ginger. Heat as prescribed and pour through a strainer into the tub of water.

For the Feet

The function of the ginger bath is to promote good circulation. When the feet become hot and red, the entire body circulation improves. Seriously ill patients too weak to stand or sit can remain on their backs and place their feet in the bowl containing the ginger mixture.

For the Body

The bath has always proved very helpful for arthritic people with pain in different parts of the body. It is also good for gout and bursitis (inflammation in the joints).

Note: If you have a heart condition of any kind, please consults with your physician before soaking in a ginger bath.

Ginger Compress

The ginger compress is the typical concept of "clean" medicine. It makes few demands of its user and takes only a few minutes to prepare. It is painless and even rather pleasant, costs little – the price of a few pounds of ginger – and accomplishes a lot. One could write a book simply recording case histories of its successes; it would be boring.

You will find it helpful in time of uncertainty as to the proper procedure for treating, especially stubborn conditions. A practical solution to various problems, it is an excellent pain reliever and a good antidote for inflammations. With its help, a cancer tumor may shrink and eventually disappear. Even internal organs and the body in general will benefit from this treatment. The ginger compress will become a friend on whom you can always depend.

Use the following basic ginger recipe as a soak or as a compress. It assists the body in healing by increasing blood circulation directly to the affected area. It also causes heat to penetrate deep within and among muscle fiber; as it radiates back to the surface, capillaries and pores stay open. This is how to use heat to carry heat away from inflammation; this is yang energy used in addressing stagnation of Ki.

Because surface heat alone may cause muscles to contract, this deeper penetration is preferable. This deeper penetration is also for bone spurs and arthritic calcification. This treatment is cumulative in its effect; continue twice a day for the needed time.

PREPARATION

Compress

Grate the ginger root, chop in a food processor, cut into tiny pieces with a sharp knife, place on a train track; you need to expose as much surface as possible – given the tools at your command.

Bring a quart of water to a boil, reduce the heat considerably and add a good fistful of grated/chopped/smashed ginger, cover and let stew for about twenty minutes.

In my household, we will put a pound or so of ginger through the food processor, scoop fistfuls of chopped ginger into baggies and place in the freezer. Always assured of plenty of ginger when needed.

The test for the efficacy of the compress or soak is that twenty minutes after completion of the treatment, the area should have a sense of warmth, the skin should look rosy, or the tissue should feel "gingery." If none of these signs show, the ginger is weak and the amount used should be increased.

This mix can be used twice (reheated once for a second dosage), then it should be discarded and a new batch made. Do this treatment at least twice a day. For a larger and stronger brew, use two quarts of water and eight ounces of grated ginger.

For a delightful and healing bath, pour this prepared mixture into a tub of hot water, climb in and sigh.

Ginger Compress # 1

· 1 quart of water
· 5 ounces grated ginger
· Have ready:
· A large bowl, two wash clothes
· Optional: aluminum foil and dry towel
  Heat water to 158 degrees Fahrenheit (70 degrees Celsius).

Do not boil! Boiling will destroy the ginger's value.

Grate the ginger and place it in a cloth bag, preferably cheesecloth. Wrap and tie the cloth bag with a string; put the cloth bag containing the ginger into the hot water. Simmer until the water is pale yellow, about twenty minutes. Remove from heat and transfer into bowl.

While it is still in the water, squeeze the bag slightly with your hand to extract the ginger.

Soak the washcloths in the very hot ginger water; remove one, squeeze out some of the liquid, and place on the affected area. The water should be as hot as the patient can tolerate.

You can cover the cloth with aluminum foil and top with the dry towel. This keeps the moist heat directed toward the site in need of attention and holds the heat in.

When the cloth begins to cool, replace and continue rotating the cloths to maintain a consistent temperature on the skin. Eventually the skin should become red. When this happens, the treatment is complete.

A person with a strong constitution will redden within ten minutes; a person with a weaker constitution will redden after twenty or thirty minutes of compress application.

For weaker patients, it may be necessary to reheat the water once or twice, being careful not to bring it to a boil. Red skin indicates the promotion of good circulation. Bedridden people will usually need repeated treatment.

For a serious, painful problem, use the ginger compress followed by an albi plaster, four to five times a day, changing after four hours. The pain will be relieved after the blood starts flowing through the vessels and efficient circulation is re-established.

Compared with deeper problems, such as stomach or uterus pain, surface problems are very easy to cure. Asthma, arthritis and nerve pain are often relatively easy to address.

Ginger Compress # 2

· 3-4 tablespoons fresh grated ginger root to 1 quart of water
or
· 4-6 tablespoons of quality medicinal grade ginger root powder to 1 quart of water
Bring water to a boil, reduce to a simmer, add the ginger, cover and simmer for twenty minutes.

Have ready: A large bowl, two wash clothes

If using powdered ginger, be sure to break up the lumps (a fork works if you do not have a whisk) and ensure the ginger powder and water are thoroughly blended. Cover and simmer for twenty minutes. Use mixture as hot as you can tolerate without burning yourself. Dip in a heavy cloth, wring and apply to muscles of the extremities and areas of the trunk, such as the abdomen, low back, mid-back, upper back, shoulders, neck and chest.

When skin begins to cool, re-dip and re-apply cloth. Repeat until the skin holds a bright red color or mixture becomes cool.

Ginger Juice

The juice of the ginger root is an ingredient in many recipes: beverages, food, and external treatments. To make ginger juice, simply grate ginger with a Japanese grater or regular grater, using the side that produces the finest consistency. Press the shavings through cheesecloth or simply squeeze by hand or use a garlic press. If you have a juicer, life is easier.

Ginger Oil

Place grated ginger in a jar and cover the ginger with sesame or olive oil. Cover the jar and shake several times a day for three days, then strain.

Mix equal parts grated ginger juice and sesame or olive oil and massage into the skin for pain in muscles or spine. The effect is equal to that of a ginger compress and sometimes stronger.

This is a very helpful remedy for headaches, pain in the spine or joints, muscle pain, earache, and scalp disease resulting in dandruff or baldness. Refrigerate if you want it to last more than two or three days.

To treat earache, place two or three drops of the ginger oil mixture on a piece of cotton and press into the aching ear, keeping the head tipped sideways for a while until the mixture has penetrated the ear. Keep the oiled piece of cotton in the ear hole for a few hours.

For dandruff, make enough of this mixture to rub on the entire scalp. Apply at night; keep on for at least eight hours. It is even better to keep the mixture on throughout the following day and then wash with an herbal shampoo. Try this a few times, such as twice a week for a month.

The ginger oil recipe with one part oil to one part ginger (1:1) is the strongest decoction. Weaker mixtures would be 2:1 or 3:1. As needed.

GREEN CABBAGE PLASTER

A reasonable substitute if no albi/taro is available

PREPARATION

Grind a head of green cabbage* in a blender or food processor. This is 70 percent of the ingredients. Add 25 percent flour and 5 percent grated ginger. Add enough water to make a thick paste.

Apply to affected area, using gauze or cheesecloth. Change in two hours and every four to six hours thereafter.

Apply a fresh plaster before going to bed.

*May substitute green plant leaves, such as radish tops, Swiss chard, parsley, watercress, or grass. *See Chlorophyll Plaster.*

HIJIKI

Hijiki is a sea vegetable rich in calcium, iron and magnesium. It has been in the Japanese diet for centuries. It is rich in dietary fiber and is considered an aid in skin beauty and luxurious hair.

USES

Medicinally, hijiki is consumed to prevent high blood pressure and maintain the thyroid gland. Health benefits of hijiki include its health influence on the digestive system; it boosts energy levels and strengthen bones.

PREPARATION

The woman who gave me these next two recipes was very close to O-Sensei. When he and I were creating a newsletter in 1986, he asked her for a couple of simple nutritional recipes. I include them as a sign of gratitude and respect.

· 1 cup hijiki (dried)
· ½ medium size onion
· 1 small carrot
· 3 tablespoons shaved bonito (dried, fermented, and smoked skipjack tuna)
· 5 tablespoons soy sauce
· 1 tablespoon corn oil

Soften hijiki in water for about ten minutes. Cut the onion and carrot in very thin slices.

Pour one tablespoon of oil into frying pan. Put onion, carrot and shaved bonito in frying pan and cook with medium heat until it softens.

When the vegetables are partially cooked, add the hijiki and stir adequately. Then add the soy sauce, stir thoroughly and removed from heat.

KIM CHI

Kim chi is a traditional Korean dish of fermented vegetables, the most common consists of fermented chili peppers, cabbage and daikon radish; though a variety of vegetables may be used in Kimchi. Eaten fresh or fermented (store at room temperature for 1 to 5 months). It is a side dish at nearly every Korean meal.

USES

It contains "healthy bacteria" called lactobacilli, found in fermented foods like kimchi, miso and yogurt. This healthful bacterium aids digestion and seems to help stop and even prevent yeast infections. Some studies show fermented cabbage has compounds that may prevent the growth of cancer.

PREPARATION

· 1 tablespoon red chile powder
· 1 tablespoon grated garlic
· 1 tablespoon ginger juice (from grated fresh ginger)
· 1 tablespoon raw or brown sugar
· 1 tablespoon tiny shrimp in salt (from Oriental grocery store)
· 3 tablespoons (approximately) sliced green scallions
· 1 teaspoon sea salt
· 4 inches (approximately) daikon (white) radish
· 1 bunch Chinese cabbage
· 1 tablespoon sea salt

Cut the white daikon radish in small strips lengthwise. Lay these strips flat and slice lengthwise again, as you would to julienne carrots. Cover these strips with salt "and mix nicely." The salt will soften the daikon.

Mix in the red chile and blend until the daikon turns pink. Add sugar, garlic, ginger juice, onion and tiny shrimp small dried fish may be substituted for the shrimp (or the shrimp may be left out of the recipe.); blend thoroughly. Cover and set aside.

Cut the Chinese cabbage into approximately 1 ½-inch pieces. Place into a large bowl, cover with salt and mix thoroughly together. Let sit for four hours covered with a lid heavy enough to press some of the water from the cabbage. Do not refrigerate; room temperature is best. After four hours, softly squeeze excess water from the cabbage and discard the water.

Place the cabbage back into the bowl and stir in the chile mixture thoroughly. Place the Kim chi into a jar and cover it tightly. Store in a cool, dark place for two to three weeks; longer is better. Serve as desired.

KUZU ROOT

Kuzu is processed from a very deep root (perhaps three or four feet long) that grows in Japan. Imported to the United States for erosion control and called kudzu, its vines now cover over seven million acres in the southeast states. It is spreading at an annual rate of 150,000 acres.

Most health food stores now carry it. In the Japanese kitchen, it is the main ingredient in pudding recipes and is used as a thickener in gravies and other uses much like the uses of cornstarch and flour.

USES

Healing qualities include curing colds and sore throats, healing weak intestines, neutralizing acidity, alleviating body pain and relaxing tight muscles.

When my daughter, Dasya, was eleven, our family came down with a respiratory flu, everyone except Dasya. She made us a kuzu/ginger concoction that was incredible! She recommended "as much ginger as you can handle." I call her concoction, "Dasya's Killer Kuzu." Try it for throat and lung issues. You will like it. Kuzu/soy tea is effective for digestive system issues, while kuzu mixed with soy, plum, bancha and ginger has proven very effective against cold, diarrhea and stomach cramps.

PREPARATION

To use kuzu, it is best to first use a mortar and pestle and reduce the kuzu to a fine powder.

Basic Recipe
· 1 teaspoon kuzu powder
· ¾ cup water
· A pinch of grated ginger

Put a few drops of water in the powdered kuzu and dissolve it to a thick slurry consistency. (If you do not first dilute with a few drops of water, the kuzu powder will form powder balls and you will never get it dissolved.) In a saucepan, dilute the kuzu slurry in the rest of the water. Place over low heat on the stove, stirring constantly. The mixture will change from chalky white to opaque to clear. When it turns clear, remove from heat and stir in the ginger. If you allow it to get past clear, it will thicken and lose its medicinal value. Drink this brew as hot as you can tolerate.

Kuzu/Soy Tea

· 1 teaspoon of kuzu powder
· Half-cup water (4 ounces)
· 1 enthusiastic dash of soy sauce

Completely dissolve kuzu in one teaspoon of cold water (make into a thick paste). Add remainder of water. Place over low heat, simmer until clear and then remove immediately. Add the dash of soy sauce and continue stirring for a minute or so. It should be thick but in liquid form. Let cool slightly. Drink all at once.

For digestive issues, take kuzu one hour before meals, preferably in the morning with an empty stomach. Try for two or three mornings.

Kuzu/Ginger Tea

· 1 teaspoon of kuzu
· ½ cup of water (4 ounces)
· 1 pinch freshly grated ginger

Completely dissolve kuzu in one teaspoon of cold water and make into a thick paste. Add remainder of water. Place over low heat, simmer until clear, and then remove immediately. Stir in ginger. Drink while hot (warm).

Alternative with ginger juice: For sore throat, keep the flame very low, heat till kuzu is clear, add half a teaspoon ginger juice and continue stirring for a minute or so. It should be thick but in liquid form. You may add honey. Sip it while it is still warm.

Kuzu Soy Plum Bancha Ginger ("Kuzu Acute")

· 1 salt plum (umeboshi)
· 10 drops juice from grated ginger (approximately)
· 1 tablespoon soy sauce
· 1 rounded tablespoon kuzu
· 1 cup bancha tea

Dissolve the kuzu in a little of the bancha tea. Heat the remaining tea and add the dissolved kuzu. Cook preparation on low heat until it becomes clear; this should be only a few seconds. Add salt plum, soy sauce and ginger juice. Stir over heat two to three minutes. Drink it hot on an empty stomach. Do not eat for an hour or so after drinking.

Use for colds, diarrhea, and stomach cramps.

MISO

Miso looks like a paste. It is salty. Its spicy flavor enhances soups and various other dishes. I have read that the traditional Japanese household has at least 360 miso recipes and, typically, the household consumes miso once or twice a day. A serving is one teaspoon. A serving for me is one tablespoon.

There are three types of miso: hatcho, mugi and kome. Hatcho miso is made of soybeans with no grains; it is aged three years in wooden barrels. Mugi is made of barley and soybeans; it is aged eighteen months. Kome is made with soybeans and rice and is aged six months. In Japan, kome is the most popular type of miso. Hatcho is quite strong for everyday use, especially in the summer. It is advisable for those how have not developed a taste for miso to start with mugi or kome. Misos can be mixed.

Dark miso has a larger soybean portion. Dark miso is saltier; the lighter miso is sweeter. Dark miso is excellent for wintertime dishes; light, sweet miso is great in the summer for soups, sauces, dips and salad dressings.

USES

Anemia, arthritis, intestinal issues, cancer, high blood pressure, arteriosclerosis, and menopause discomfort can all be treated with miso, and miso can be used to offset the detrimental effects of meat, sugar and soft drinks.

Miso is the original "probiotic," valued for its beneficial effects on intestinal bacteria because it replenishes the microflora that lives in the digestive tract and is destroyed by antibiotics. A cup of miso daily while taking antibiotics restores the lost bacteria.

Miso is also valuable in battling cancer. Breast, ovarian, prostate and other estrogen-sensitive cancers are quite responsive to genistein, an isoflavone in miso. Many clinical studies found malignant tumors reduced by consuming miso. It is considered a preventive food for avoiding cancer. Menopause symptoms also respond to miso.

Miso aids in preventing arteriosclerosis and high blood pressure because it dissolves cholesterol in the blood.

In addition, miso helps address acidity in the blood caused by the high phosphorus content of meat, sugar and soft drinks. Phosphorus leaches calcium and other minerals from bone to restore the natural state of alkalinity that our blood needs for proper health and longevity. Stay calm and keep the blood alkaline.

Hatcho is excellent for detoxifying yeast and candida; however, sugar and sweet tasting foods must be eliminated.

PREPARATION

Because of miso's powerful ability to absorb toxins, it is better that you transfer it from its plastic container to a glass, wooden or ceramic container for storage.

Miso is a live food and boiling destroys the beneficial enzymes. When making healing dishes, add the miso a minute or two before removing from the heat.

Miso Soup

Miso soup is a precious part of the Japanese food tradition. It is an excellent alkalizer and helps promote proper metabolism. Its other properties include providing or improving resistance to sickness and, because it contains natural enzymes, aiding in the digestion and assimilation of food. It is high in proteins, amino acids and vitamin B-12. Miso assists in detoxing drugs, radiation, alcohol, nicotine and excessive animal fats. For this reason, it may be taken once daily by those who feel they need it.

Miso Broth

- 2 tablespoons chopped scallions
- 2 teaspoons mugi miso (barley)
- 1 cup hot water

Puree scallions and miso. Gradually add hot water, stirring constantly. Drink immediately. Michio Kushi, a contemporary of Masahilo Nakazono Osensei, recommended this drink for early stages of a cold or headache. It stimulates circulation and may induce sweating.

Recipe # 1

Proportions (using the onion/cabbage combination*):

- 2 onions minced
- ½ cabbage, shredded
- 1 tablespoon oil (sunflower or sesame)
- 4 cups of water
- 6 rounded teaspoons miso paste

Sauté the vegetables in oil and simmer ten to fifteen minutes. Boil water and pour into the deep pot in which the vegetable has just been sautéed. Cover, bring to a boil, reduce heat and simmer thirty minutes. Dilute miso in one cup of the simmering broth and add to mixture five minutes before the end of cooking. Do not boil soup after adding miso. That will make it bitter and destroy its nutritional and healing properties. Stir well. You may serve miso soup with finely chopped scallions sprinkled on top. In warm months, you may add small cubes of tofu. (Tofu is cooling to the stomach.)

*Several combinations of vegetables are commonly used. The most popular are

- Daikon (Japanese radish)/Wakame (seaweed)
- Daikon greens/Wakame
- Turnip/Turnip greens/Wakame
- Cauliflower/Cauliflower greens
- Onions/Wakame
- Onions/Cabbage

· Onions/Dulce (seaweed)
· Onions/Swiss chard
Recipe # 2:

The Japanese woman who gave me this recipe was very close to O-Sensei. When he and I were creating a newsletter in 1986, he asked her for a couple of simple nutritional recipes. This is one of them.

· 3 tablespoons miso paste
· ½ package of tofu, cut into cubes
· 4 cups water
· 3 tablespoons shaved bonito
· 1 green onion stems, minced

Put water and bonito in a medium sauce pan and bring to a boil. Reduce heat and add miso. Then, slowly add the cubed tofu. When the tofu has floated to the top, turn off the heat and add the green onion.

MOCHI

Mochi is Japanese rice cake made of short grain glutinous rice that is sweeter than common rice. The rice is pounded in a bowl; therefore, it is necessary to use a strong bowl that will not break or chip. To pound the rice, you will need a large wooden pestle. You will also need a steamer.

USES

Mochi is very popular in Japan. It works miracles. Japanese people recommended it for variety of sicknesses. Excellent for convalescents and breastfeeding mothers, it provides strength for the weak and abundant milk for the newborn baby. Children like it in all forms. It is especially recommended for anemia because it is a good body builder and easy to digest.

A combination of mochi and mugwort is good for leukemia and anemia patients.

PREPARATION

Wash and rinse sweet rice until water is no longer cloudy. Soak for twenty-four hours then steam rice until soft (approximately two to three hours for brown sweet rice). Next, pound until all grains are broken. Finally shape into balls, patties or squares. You may eat mochi right after it has been pounded.

After about twelve hours, it becomes hard; after several days, mochi dried in the shade becomes hard as a rock. When baked, or fried, the result is rice cakes.

It can be baked, toasted, deep-fried, and boiled. These methods improve its flavor. Add to soup before eating. There are many recipes on the Internet.

To make mugwort mochi, follow the instructions for mocha but add mugwort when you are pounding the rice. Whether the mugwort used is fresh or dry, lightly cook before adding to the rice.

MOXA/MUGWORT

Mugwort, the common name for plants in the genus Artemisia, is an aromatic plant used as an herb as well as medicine. It grows worldwide at low altitudes in sandy gravel and riverbeds. Mugwort is an organic source of iron and calcium.

Use mugwort picked in the spring when the whole plant is tender. The top of the plant picked in summer or autumn is fine too, if it is very soft.

To preserve, boil the soft part of the mugwort leaves in salt water. Dry the leaves by leaving them lying flat. Allow them to dry completely. They will keep for one or two years.

Moxibustion, the thermal therapy originated in the Far East, uses the product of cleaning and crushing the dried leaves of common mugwort, Artemisia vulgaris.

USES

Mugwort benefits people whose conditions are weak. It is helpful for heart, stomach and intestinal problems. Effective against internal bleeding, it builds blood, reduces fever, and is excellent nourishment for pregnant women. It decreases the permeability of the capillaries and increases the capability of blood coagulation.

A combination of mochi (sweet rice) and mugwort is good for leukemia and anemia patients. For leukemia, include mugwort, brown rice, buckwheat and a few cooked vegetables in the diet. Mugwort is also good for cancer patients.

Mugwort is used extensively by traditional doctors for nearly all the ills humans endure from itch to sterility. It is commonly used in the practice of acupuncture and meridian therapy. In addition, it is used in spiritual and religious ceremonies and as a folk remedy for good luck, long-life, and to keep evil spirits at bay.

Pieces of mugwort added to miso soup are flavorful and beneficial. They should become soft enough to eat. Mugwort leaves prepared in this manner are good for anemia and weakness.

Mugwort also has carminative (relieving flatulence or colic by expelling gas) and can allay the griping pains of indigestion and diarrhea. It can be prescribed as a decoction in hemoptysis (coughing up blood).

Noteworthy: Excitatory action on the uterus.

Caution: Excitatory action on the central nervous system may cause epileptic convulsions, if given in large dosage.

Contraindication: Not for use by people with heat in the blood caused by deficiency of yin (vital essence), yin kyo fever – a low-grade fever in a weak, chronically ill person.

Moxa has a variety of uses as a tea and a wash. Well-respected for its anti-bacterial and anti-fungicidal properties, it inhibits the growth of staphylococcus aureus, B-hemolytic, other streptococci, and E. coli. It can be used for

snake and insect bites, as a wash for all wounds and ulcers, as a counterirritant, and for cauterizing purposes. The raw herb moistened and placed on an open wound will stop the bleeding and seal the injury.

In addition, inhaled moxa smoke has inhibitory action on asthmatic spasms caused by histamine. It assists the dilation of the bronchi and is used for chronic bronchitis with various degrees of cough and asthma with sputum. Oral intake, including gargling, can reduce coughing. As a gargle, it is very effective addressing sore, raw throat symptoms.

Internal Uses:

- angina pectoris (acute or chronic)
- asthma (use as a gargle or tea)
- bitter taste stimulant
- colds and coughs and to resolve phlegm (use as a gargle or tea)
- control internal bleeding, including postpartum hemorrhage, functional bleeding of the uterus (See also Carp Soup.)
- dispel cold and relief pain
- dysentery
- dysmenorrhea
- worms
- mouth wash (use as a gargle or tea)
- nerve sedation for abnormal pain or labor pain
- upset stomach
- sore, dry throat (gargle or tea)
- sterility
- warm the meridians

External Uses:

- wash for skin rashes, itch, ulcerations, wounds and bites
- poultice for pain relief
- bandage for lacerations, abrasions and to control bleeding from an external wound

PREPARATION

Method # 1

Tea and Gargle

- 1 large pinch moxa (3 grams)
- 4-6 ounces boiling water
  Let steep twenty minutes

Method # 2

Gargle and External Wash

- 1 handful moxa (9 grams)
- 1 cup water; bring to boil; reduce to simmer
  Add herb, simmer, covered, for thirty minutes

MU #16 TEA

Developed by George Ohsawa, founder of Macrobiotics, Mu #16 tea is a powerful energy restorative beverage. It can be found through macrobiotic food sources, such as www.goldminefoods.com.

Although the ingredients can vary slightly by seller, Ohsawa's 16 ingredients were Mandarin orange peel, Japanese Parsley root, Herbaceous Peony root, Atractylis, Cinnamon, Cnicus, Licorice, Ginger root, Cyperus, Apricot kernels, Rehmannia, Coptis, Panex Ginseng, Cloves, Moulan.

USES

It is useful for respiratory ailments and cold conditions. It may be useful for the condition known in oriental medicine as blood deficiency. It addresses internal heat circulation and may be an extraordinary treatment for Raynaud's Disease and any other cold condition or heat circulation issue. It is a wonderful wintertime tea and, iced, makes a great summer time tea. It is an excellent source of iron.

This mixture contains licorice, which may be problematic if you have high blood pressure.

PREPARATION

· 24 ounces of cold water (spring or filtered).
· 1 ½ tablespoons Mu mixture or 1 large tea bag of Mu tea.
Combine water and Mu tea in a pan and bring to a boil. Immediately turn to low heat and simmer for twenty minutes uncovered.

Dose: Drink four ounces at a time, 1-3 times a day, during morning and afternoon. Until you are comfortable with the effect Mu tea has on your nervous system, it is best not to drink it after 4 p.m.

If any of the following occurs after drinking Mu tea, cut back or stop drinking it:

1) sleeplessness or insomnia

2) feeling hot and feverish without illness

3) feeling hot and sweating without exertion

4) exceedingly increased libido.

MORNING CONSTITUTION TEA

I cannot remember the source of this recipe. From Sensei? He taught us the value of burdock and ginger, as food and medicine. Maybe I learned it from one of several herbal teachers whom I have been graced to be around. Maybe I concocted it myself. Maybe I got it off the internet. I cannot remember. Simple to prepare; very helpful in a gentle manner.

USE

To adjust and normalize elimination.

PREPARATION

· A thumb size piece of ginger, grated
· A dash of licorice root, grated*
· A dash of burdock root, grated

Add to 1 liter of water, bring to boil, reduce heat, cover; cook for fifteen minutes. Drink a cup each morning

Licorice root is not recommended if you have high blood pressure, kidney or liver or heart disease, or diabetes. If using diuretics and during pregnancy, avoid licorice.

NERVI-LESS TEA

The ingredients of Nervi-less Tea – my own concoction of chamomile flowers, hops, passionflower, skullcap, valerian and sometimes bugleweed – all have sedative and calming properties. Chamomile has a long history as a remedy for anxiety and insomnia, and chamomile tea is widely available. Hops, an ingredient in beer, is used for those symptoms as well as restlessness, tension, and attention-deficit disorder, and is sometimes used to improve appetite, start breast-milk flow, and quell indigestion.

Skullcap (Scuttelaria lateriflora) is another sedative and is also used for inflammation and spasms. The skullcap label can be misleading. Western skullcap (Scuttelaria canescens), southern skullcap (Scutellaria cordifolia), marsh skullcap (Scutellaria galericulatum) should not be substituted for Scuttelaria lateriflora, the species of skullcap that has been studied for medicinal use. They are not interchangeable.

Valerian is a common remedy for sleep disorders and is also used for hysteria, excitability, headaches, and stomach upset. Some people use valerian for muscle and joint pain and menstrual cramps. Bugleweed is used to lower high levels of thyroid hormones. It is also used to treat premenstrual syndrome, breast pain, nervousness, insomnia, and bleeding, especially nosebleeds and heavy bleeding

USES
For sleeplessness, drug withdrawal, tension/anxiety or any condition needing tranquilizing.

PREPARATION
Thoroughly blend:
- · 2 ounces chamomile flowers
- · 1 ounce hops
- · 1 ounce passionflower

- 1 ounce skullcap
- 1 ounce valerian
- 1 ounce bugleweed (optional, if available)

Put ten to twelve tablespoons of the herbal mixture into a quart container; fill with boiling water and let it steep for ten to fifteen minutes.

or

Using a bamboo strainer half full of mixture; place in a cup and fill with boiling water; let steep for ten to fifteen minutes.

For Day Use

Drink four to six ounces every three hours.

For Night Use

Drink four to six ounces an hour before you go to bed and another four to six ounces an hour later, as you are getting into bed.

ONION, Roasted

As a poultice to draw out foreign objects.

PLUM SOY GINGER BANCHA DRINK

Ume' plum is a digestive aid in traditional medicine, as is ginger. This recipe is the same as Kuzu Soy Plum Bancha Tea except without the Kuzu. Kuzu calms the nerves and settles the stomach but this recipe is also helpful.

USES

This drink strengthens the heart. Traditionally, it also addresses fatigue, poor circulation and sluggish metabolism. Consume three times a day in the case of a duodenum ulcer. Good for intestinal digestion, initiates stomach activity and restores appetite.

This drink has the exceptional function of removing old salt from the organisms and supplying new salt. Ginger (yang) promotes good circulation; salt (yin) strengthens the heart when taken by itself. Ginger might create acidity when consumed raw, but the combination of both balances their energies.

PREPARATION

· ½ umeboshi plum
· 5 drop ginger juice
· 1 teaspoon soy sauce
· 1 cup bancha (Japanese Twig) tea (boiling)

Boil bancha tea; add salt plum, soy sauce, and ginger juice. Stir and leave on low heat for one minute or so. Drink it hot but not too hot.

POTATO

The potato, a starchy, tuberous crop from the perennial nightshade, Solanum, is native to the Andes but has become a major food supply throughout the world. Parts are poisonous and preparation is important. The potato contains vitamins and minerals but is best known for its carbohydrate content, primarily in the form of starch. A small but significant portion of this starch is resistant to digestion by enzymes and is considered to have health benefits similar to fiber. However, the health benefits depend on preparation.

USES

White potato can be good for stomach ulcer, duodenum ulcer, and stomach acidity. People with strong constitutions can eat potatoes.

PREPARATION

Be sure to remove the sprouts, green spots and green skin because these contain solanine, a neurotoxin. Small amounts may not adversely affect an adult but a child or a frail person could end up with vomiting, diarrhea, headaches, or central nervous system problems. If you find green sprouts, skin, or spots, throw the potato away.

To Remove Yang and Increase Yin

People with weak constitutions who wish to eat potatoes should use this special preparation, which lessens the potentially harmful effects of the potato.

Peel potatoes, sprinkle with salt and let soak for a while. Rinse and put in a pot with salted water. Cook for several hours. To make the potatoes even more yin, energetically less expansive, remove from water, slice and sprinkle with salt to draw out the liquid. Then fry in oil previously salted.

Potato Juice

Use for gastric, stomach and duodenum issues; to stop gastric pain and cure gastric ulcers. It is also good for those prone to allergies.

· One raw white potato, grated.
· 6 ounces of water
· Mix and drink daily

Better Potato Juice Recipe

Wash and grate* raw potatoes. Squeeze** through cheesecloth to remove juice.

Drink a half cup of this juice three times a day before meals.

Red potatoes are best for this, and the next best are blue-skinned potatoes. Some sources say white and yellow skin potatoes are a little less effective, although I really do not know if this is true.

For Gastric Ulcers

Grate* fresh potatoes, squeeze** and place juice in earthenware or porcelain pan. Simmer uncovered until water evaporates. This will take a long time. When evaporation is complete, only black carbon from the potatoes will remain. This is almost a complete protein. Take one teaspoon with water once a day.

*Instead of grating, chop fine in a food processor.

** Instead of squeezing, use a juicer.

PUMPKIN

Pumpkins, believed to have been initially cultivated in the Americas at least 8,000 years before Columbus, is a cultivar of squash high in vitamin A. Most parts of the pumpkin are edible, including the seeds, leaves, and flowers.

USES

Pumpkin is beneficial to the spleen and pancreas and can help with a sore throat. Both the pulp and the seeds can help with eliminating worms and parasites.

PREPARATION

For trouble with the spleen or the pancreas, cook pumpkin or squash with adzuki beans. Eat one cup every day

For throat trouble, pain, or excess mucous, baked pumpkin is good. The same results are obtained with a tea made by boiling pumpkin seeds in water (twenty seeds to two cups of water).

Both cooked pumpkin and roasted pumpkin seeds are effective in expelling worms and parasites. Pumpkin leaves are useful as well.

RANSHIO

Ranshio is a very strong mixture of egg and soy sauce; therefore, it is most important to evaluate carefully the patient's condition and strength before administering it. To prevent a strong and sudden reaction, it is highly advisable to administer this mixture a little at a time, spoonful by spoonful. Nor should it be used too often. If regular treatment is needed, egg oil rather than ranshio is recommended.

USES

Ranshio is used in extreme cases of excess yang energy toxicity, for example, when a person's pupils rise, revealing the whites of the eye on three sides (sanpaku). Eyes turn upward because of extreme yang presence in the organism. This preparation will immediately restore the pupils to their normal position. The yin ranshio produces a strong contraction that brings the patient back to normal.

Persons have used this with much success treating heart failure resulting from a weak condition. If symptoms indicate the patient's condition is yin, ranshio might be given.

Indications: Heart failure, overly weak heart, weak kidney energy, yang convulsions (often aggravated by too much meat in the diet); also, recommended in the treatment of snakebites.

Contraindications: In Healing Ourselves, Dr. N. Muramoto advised against a person with heart failure who has recently eaten large amounts of animal protein from taking Ranshio.

PREPARATION

Ranshio has only two ingredients: egg and soy sauce;

Mixed in a ratio of 4:1 – One raw fertile egg mixed 4 to 1 with tamari or soy sauce; use half the egg shell and fill it half way with soy sauce and mix.

or

Strongest Dosage: (acute care situation, ultimate yin medicine) – Mix the yoke of a raw fertile egg with slightly less than a half eggshell full of soya (or soy in the United States) sauce.

Dosage: Take one teaspoon at a time. Use carefully and sparingly.

THIS IS A VERY POWERFUL TREATMENT. GIVE ONLY ONCE A DAY

RICE (Brown)

Brown rice, found in only health food stores a few years ago, has made its way into the American market. Until recently, brown rice lay on the shelves and was sold in small packages as if it were a food to be eaten once in a great while. Now it is being purchased by the 100-pound bag. It is a complete staple food, rich in minerals and vitamins and indispensable to good health.

USES

Rice is good for the lungs and the colon. Short grain is better for colder weather, medium or long for summer. Sweet brown rice is good for pregnant women, nursing mothers and children.

PREPARATION

Brown rice can be cooked in many ways but the most convenient is simmering. This method retains more vitamins and minerals and results in better flavor.

Wash the pot and fill with a desired mount of rice and water. Try not to fill more than half the pot, otherwise the rice might fail to cook well or may even over flow. It might also burn because of insufficient water. Use one cup of rice with one and two-third cups of water.

Cover and set over a high flame. When the water reaches a rolling boil, lower the flame to simmering point. Let it cook for fifty minutes or so. If the rice burns, it might be that the flame was too high during the simmering period or that there was not enough water. Lower the flame a bit next time. If the rice is wet or uncooked, the flame might have been too low. If the rice is mushy, too much water was used. Do not remove cover while cooking. Leave it on until five minutes after rice has finished cooking.

Soft Rice

To make soft rice, use more water (1/2 times more) than for cooking regular rice. Simmer for two hours. Soft rice is good for people with delicate stomach and intestines.

Rice Cream

Rice cream sprinkled with sesame salt is excellent for breakfast, especially in winter. It is available in all health food stores. Be sure to buy it fresh. If not available, make it yourself in a flour mill or flour blender. (Do not grind as thin as flour; it should be slightly coarse). To grind the rice yourself, wash the rice, then rinse and toast over a high medium flame in a large cast iron skillet. While toasting it, be careful to stir continuously and fast enough to prevent burning. It should not take more than ten minutes to toast one cup of rice. Then grind.

(for 2-3 people)
· 5 tablespoon roasted ground rice
· 4 cups of water
· ¼ teaspoon salt

Mix ground rice with cold water. Stir over high flame until mixture comes to a boil. Add salt, cover and simmer for thirty minutes. During that period, stir two or three times to prevent burning.

Rice Milk

It is very easy to make rice milk. Simply cook rice with water seven times its volume (one cup rice, seven cups water) for two hours over a low flame, covered. When rice is finished cooking, place the solid rice grain in cheesecloth and squeeze the liquid through by twisting the cheesecloth. Continue until all liquid is extracted and only pulp remains in the cheesecloth (this pulp can be used in baking bread).

After this juice has been separated from the pulp, it should be cooked again for ten minutes to two hours, depending on the consistency desired. For babies or very weak people, it should have a thin consistency, for stronger people it should be thicker. Rice milk may be feed to babies when the mother cannot produce enough milk. Rice milk is an excellent remedy for gastric intestinal trouble. It is advisable to take this food exclusively in the event of severe gastric trouble.

Rice Water, Soup, Milk, and Cream

· 1 cup whole brown rice (washed well)
· 15 cups of water
  Cook eight to ten hours over very low heat. Do not boil!! (You may need to add more water during cooking.)

1. After cooking, drain the rice. Save liquid and rice pulp.
2. Press rice pulp through a sieve. Save liquid and rice pulp.

The liquid from #1 is "rice water."

The liquid from #2 is "rice soup".

The liquid from #1 and #2 mixed together is "rice milk."

The pressed pulp from #2 is "rice cream."

Mix the liquid and rice cream, as needed. Keep refrigerated.

SALT BANCHA

Bancha is a green tea made from leaves harvested later in the season or from lower shoots on the plant. Its leaves are larger and coarser and it has a strong straw smell. Bancha tea typically has less caffeine and amino acids than other green tea.

USES

Bancha tea has antioxidant benefits.

Externally, with a dash of sea salt added, it can help relieve eye pain or can be used as a gentler substitute for a ginger compress.

PREPARATION

Heat one cup of bancha tea and add a pinch of salt. This simple preparation can prove very helpful when used as a substitute for the ginger compress. Sometimes a ginger compress is too strong for a tender area. For example, to relieve eye pain, put lukewarm salt bancha in an eyeglass and let the painful eye (leave the eyes open!) bathe in a salty liquid for a few seconds. Renew the liquid and repeat a few more times. To help cure either nearsightedness or farsightedness, follow this treatment with the application of an albi plaster every night for a week. (Place a layer of gauze between plaster and eye.)

SEA VEGETABLES

Incorporate into your stews, soups and imagination. The various sea vegetables, "seaweed" detoxify lead, all heavy metals, chemical pollutants, and radiation.

In a compress, sea vegetables have cooling properties.

SESAME

Sesame seed, one of the oldest oilseed crops with among the highest oil contents, has many species, most being wild and native to sub-Saharan Africa. It has a rich, nutty flavor and is a common ingredient in cuisines across the world.

Sesame seeds are high in nutritional content, including vitamins, minerals, natural oils, and organic compounds, including calcium, iron, magnesium, phosphorous, manganese, copper, zinc, fiber, thiamin, vitamin B6, folate, protein, and tryptophan.

Sesame Oil

USES

Sesame oil consumed internally moistens the intestines. Sesame oil externally treats rheumatism.

Use as a lotion on skin for chafing, dryness, abrasions, sun burn, wind burn. Rubbing sesame oil on a scar might reduce its size. For tired eyes to scratched cornea, place a drop of oil that is body temperature on the eye; blink to distribute oil and then continue blinking periodically for thirty minutes. Do not attempt to read, drive a vehicle, or watch television for that thirty minutes. Don't fall asleep either, it may result in your eyelids getting stuck closed.

PREPARATION

Black sesame oil is preferred; dark roasted is acceptable. The oil should be purified. Place oil in a pan over heat. Cook until it begins to smoke; remove from heat. This removes water and impurities.

Sesame Salt

Sesame salt (gomashio) consists of different proportions of salt and sesame seed; from 1:5 to 1:10 (one part salt to ten parts sesame seeds). Some people even use 1:12. First try 1:8 and see if it is too strong for you. You can change the proportions per your taste and needs.

PREPARATION

Use unbleached sesame seeds. Wash the seeds, rinse, and toast in a heavy cast iron skillet. Stir constantly with a wooden spatula until the seeds begin to 'pop', about ten 'pops'; then they are done. To avoid an unpleasant after-taste, be careful not to burn any of the seeds.

Apply low heat to the salt in a cast iron pan until a faint odor of chlorine rises from the salt. Remove from fire and put into suribachi (special bowl for grinding) along with sesame seeds. Place suribachi between your legs and rotate the wooden pestle (surikogi) with both hands. Do not use pressure. Your sesame salt is ready when most of the seeds are crushed. Sprinkle on rice cream and other grains. Keep in an airtight container.

To relieve headache or heartburn, take a spoon of sesame salt. Chew well, of course. Sesame salt also can be sprinkled on rice cream and other grains.

SHISO

Shiso is the more common name of the herb perilla of the mint family. There are two kinds of shiso. One has purple leaves and stems. The other is green. The green variety is more delicious as food; it is spicy, cinnamon-like. The purple shiso serves as medicine. Shiso leaves were once known as "beefsteak leaves." The purple (or red) variety is used by the Japanese to color umeboshi and pickled ginger.

USES

Because shiso is one of the foods richest in calcium and iron, it is highly effective for bone and joint troubles and anemia. Shiso leaves are also effective for addressing fever, asthma, colds, flus, coughing and other respiratory issues, as well as stomach trouble and even complex mental conditions. For coughing, use shiso leaves as a tea. It stimulates purging of fluids, including sweating and urination, and is good for cases of food poisoning, especially fish poisoning. Chew shiso leaves to develop E Dimension, judgment.

PREPARATION

Slicing shiso leaves length-wise in thin strips (julienne) strongly enhances the anise, basil, cinnamon and spearment flavors found therein. Try in a citrus salad or mixed green salad.

Green shiso leaves are often wrapped around sushi or served with "sashimi" as a garnish. They are added to soups and tempura recipes. Dried and crumpled, it can be sprinkled over rice or over tuna or added to green tea. Enjoy. Heal.

SHIITAKE MUSHROOM

Shiitake mushroom are dried mushrooms used in Japan and China. They are now grown commercially in the United States. You can buy them now in most health food stores and grocery stores.

USES

Shiitake mushrooms are excellent medicine for the kidney and are particularly effective in discharging animal protein. Much research is going on in Japan concerning the effects of Shitake mushrooms in the treatment of cancer.

PREPARATION

Boil or soak in water and sauté, or cook in soup, especially barley soup.

SOY BANCHA TEA

USES

Soy bancha tea is a very effective drink for migraines and fatigue. Soy-ginger-umeboshi with bancha or kukicha tea is an excellent internal treatment for stomach cramps, although a more lasting cure is a balanced diet with grains that provide vitamin B, which supports the nervous system.

PREPARATION

· 1 cup bancha tea
· 1 teaspoon soy sauce

Heat the tea and stir in the soy sauce. Let simmer a few seconds. Take it hot but not too hot.

Soy-Ginger-Umeboshi with Bancha or Kukicha Tea

· 1 cup bancha or kukicha tea
· 1 pinch of grated ginger
· 1 umeboshi plum

Heat the tea, stir in the soy sauce and add the salt plum. Let simmer 30 seconds. Sip it hot but not too hot.

SPINACH

Spinach is an edible plant in the family Amaranthaceae, native to central and western Asia. It is believed to have originated in ancient Persia, then introduced to India and eventually China.

USES

Spinach is a nutrient-dense food that lowers the risk of cancer and is excellent for health of skin, hair and bone. Its high fiber aids digestion, and it helps lower blood pressure. t is very rich in vitamins, minerals and protein – a lot of protein. Most of its calories come from its protein; however, my universe doesn't care about "calories" or "protein" so you can ignore the last sentence. It digests easily, thus, is very good for infants and ill persons.

PREPARATION

Spinach Oshitashi

The Japanese woman who gave me this recipe was very close to Sensei. When he and I were creating a newsletter in 1986, he asked her for a couple of simple nutritional recipes. I include them as a sign of gratitude and respect.

Ingredients: (Serves four)

· 1 bunch of spinach
· 3 tablespoons of shaved bonito
· Soy sauce – the amount that suits you.
Wash the spinach thoroughly. Bring water in a medium saucepan to a boil. Add the spinach, bring the water back to a boil, and cook two to three minutes, uncovered.

Quickly cool the spinach with running water. Remove excess water; place in a serving dish, sprinkle with shaved bonito and a bit of soy sauce.

TOFU COMPRESS

Tofu slabs are useful for first aid in emergencies and illness involving inflammation, fever, traumatic soft tissue injury and head trauma. As a traditional treatment for cerebral vascular accidents (stroke), a half-inch layer of tofu is applied to the patient's shaved head within two days of the stroke. The tofu is changed repeatedly as it dries or changes color. See also Tofu Plaster.

Slice a quarter to half inch-thick slab of tofu. Use where needed. Turn slab over when its color changes to yellow; change when it dries or turns yellow on both sides.

TOFU PLASTER

Tofu plaster treatment may be quite effective for cerebral hemorrhage if applied within forty-eight hours of the time the cerebral vascular accident occurs. After that time, a blood clot will most likely have formed, making the cure extremely difficult. In such a case, cut the hair close to the scalp (shave, if possible) and apply tofu plaster. If paralysis has set on one side, apply the plaster to the alternate side of the head. If blindness has set in, apply plasters to both sides.

This may be somewhat effective.

This type of plaster is best for head wounds, concussions, headache, fever, earache and cerebral hemorrhage, although probably chlorophyll and albi plasters may be used with the same effectiveness.

· 80 percent tofu
· 15 percent wheat flour
· 5 percent ginger (if available, grated or powder)
Put tofu in a clean cheesecloth and gently squeeze out the water. Next, place the squeezed tofu in a bowl and add the flour. Mix thoroughly. Put the mixture on a clean cheesecloth, spreading it evenly, about ¼ inch thick. Bandage in place.

Change every two hours, or when it dries half way, or when it turns yellow, whichever comes first.

For cerebral hemorrhage and other very serious incidences, change the plaster every thirty minutes. Maintain this routine constantly for a period of at least one week. Tofu is recommended because it is slow to harden and is thus best for healing internal bleeding.

UME/UMEBOSHI

Ume' is a Japanese fruit. It is referred to as a plum; it is in the apricot family. Umeboshi (Japanese Salt Plums) are ume plums that have been pickled in salt for more than two years by a special acid bacterial process. They are sweet, sour and salty. Salt plums have many uses in the ancient Japanese pharmacopoeia. Their place in the kitchen is central. They enhance various dishes, sometimes serving as a dressing, replacing vinegar, sometimes to alkalize some acidic dishes. Sometimes to act as they are, a pickled fruit. They are pickled for a minimum of one month; three years is recommended. Umeboshi aged fifteen years tastes quite mild.

USES
As medicine, the umeboshi plum works miracles. Stomachaches, stomach cramps, certain types of headache, including migraines, and acidity are some of the minor issues these plums can relieve. They also counteract fatigue and act as a preventive of dysentery.

The seed of the umeboshi also has multiple usages; sucking on the seed addresses nausea and can provide relief for thirstiness or "dry mouth." It has been recorded that taping the seed to the navel may help morning sickness. While it is worth the try, ume concentrate is THE remedy for morning sickness.

PREPARATION
Salted plums are usually sold packed in shiso (beefsteak leaves), an herb high in calcium and an important ingredient in many of the herbal tea recipes. If the plums seem too dry, they can be soaked in water before use. Salt plum juice, which is also a very effective medicine, is at the bottom of the crock, keg or jar.

Ume Plum Beverage

· 1 umeboshi plum
· 1 quart of water
    Simmer gently for one hour. Take as appropriate, with each meal or every three to four hours, to address stomach or intestinal discomfort. This beverage is excellent cooled, as a summer tea.

Ume' Plum Concentrate

Ume' Plum Concentrate helps balance the PH in the digestive system and neutralize acidity. It is a reduction of fresh ume' plums. Called bainiku ekisu in Japan, this 50X concentrate is a reduction of one kilo of fresh ume' plums to twenty grams of thick dark paste. The concentrate is thirty times the strength of umeboshi, without the sodium. Physicians, athletes, and emperors have wisely used this balancing and bracing gift of the vegetable kingdom for centuries. It is useful in addressing many conditions and situations:

· Candida and other fungal conditions, including thrush and toe-nail fungus.
· Constipation, diarrhea
· Crohn's disease, irritable bowel syndrome.
· Headaches, migraines, vertigo, sinus issues
· Morning sickness, nausea, vomiting
· Stomach-ache, stomach flu
· "Morning after the night before"
· Jet lag
· Feeling "acidic," being acidic
· Food poisoning
· Mouth sores
    Many, many issues

Ume Tea

Dissolve one soybean-sized drop of ume concentrate in two to three ounces of warm water. Traditionally, use a chopstick to draw out a dollop of ume. It need not be dissolved or diluted; it can be consumed directly.

Take as needed:

With each meal.

Every three to four hours.

Drink one to two times per day.

When there is stomach or intestinal discomfort.

WATERMELON

Originally from southern Africa, where it still grows wild, watermelon is a kind of berry in the same family as cucumber, squash and pumpkin. China is now the world's single largest watermelon producer. Buy local. Grow your own.

USES

Watermelon is especially therapeutic for kidney and bladder issues. Watermelon cleanses the kidneys. It is anti-inflammatory. It is used in addressing obesity, diabetes and heart disease. It is said to promote healthy hair, complexion and increase energy.

Eating watermelon aids in removing old salt from the system, unless you dump salt all over your watermelon before consuming it.

Watermelon syrup can reduce blood pressure in obese middle-aged adults with prehypertension or stage 1 hypertension. Watermelon extract improves arterial function.

PREPARATION

Watermelon Syrup Extract

Squeeze the red pulp of the watermelon to extract the juice. Boil this liquid until thick. Dilute one tablespoon of syrup in one cup of water and take two times a day at least thirty minutes before meals.

TREATMENT BY SYMPTOMS

ARTHRITIS-TYPE* SYMPTOMS

Treatment:

1. Eliminate all sugar from your diet. Decreasing sweets helps but eliminating them helps a lot more. This means no sweets: no pies, cakes, pastry, ice cream, or sodas. For full rehabilitation, avoid all sweeteners, including corn syrup, maple syrup, honey, fructose, artificial sweeteners, and "natural" sweeteners. Do you want to get rid of your discomfort or what?

2. Decrease fat intake. Less meat of all kinds, cut back on oils, salad dressings, all forms of dairy, avoid fried foods, margarine and other fats.

3. Decrease caffeine, especially coffee and caffeine "enhanced" beverages. One cup of quality coffee daily might be okay, more than one may be troublesome. (Nakazono Osensei found that three cups of coffee in a week aggravated his arthritis.) Be leery of chocolate and cocoa and restrict your use of aspirin.

4. Take a minimum of 2,000 mgs of vitamin C daily.

5. Take 400 IU's (international units) of vitamin E daily.

6. Eat an abundance of green vegetables. Arthritis indicates fever in the intestines. Greens will help cool the fire in your guts.

This is your body; be kind, be patient. It takes a long time for these symptoms to appear. It will take a while for them to disappear. Just following these directions alone should bring relief within four to six months.

With meridian therapy, soaks (see recipes), additional nutritional considerations (white flour products are inflammatory; sweet potatoes are anti-inflammatory) and more aggressive self-health care, this time can be reduced significantly.

Any word that ends with "itis" is an inflammation issue. Follow this guideline.

ASTHMA

Yin type asthma remedies include juice from grated radish mixed with yinnie syrup* or honey. Yin asthmatic people should eat more vegetables.

People with yang type asthma are pale. They should cut down on liquids and eat more whole grains and other yin quality foods, especially brown rice. Root vegetables are good and lotus is especially effective. Lotus has long been used as a lung medicine. Lotus root is excellent sautéed; lotus seeds are good also.

Yinnie syrup is a sweetener made from rice.

BRONCHITIS, ACUTE

Internal Treatment: Daikon radish drink

External Treatment: Ginger compress and albi plaster

BURNS

A burn in the kitchen, a severe sunburn or any thermal burn, responds amazingly to immersion in a saline bath. Use sea salt dissolved in tepid water to approximate the salinity of the ocean. Immerse the burned area in this solution until the pain or discomfort is gone.

This treatment will lesson blistering and skin damage.

In addition:

· Cucumber juice externally applied to burns is an excellent treatment.
· Onion root or bulb crushed and used as an external poultice helps.
· Sesame oil is especially helpful after a burn has "calmed down."
· Slippery elm bark can also be used as a poultice.
· Soy sauce or miso applied to burn is calming.
· Tofu compress reduces burn pain and damage.

CHILLS

Treatment: Eucalyptus leaves, brewed as a strong tea

Drink a half to one teacupful three times a day. Sipping is very useful. You may sweeten with a little local honey.

COLIC

Treatment: Fennel seeds and leaves, brewed as a tea

A spoonful to a cup of boiling water. Steep twenty minutes. Wineglassful every half hour as needed

The most powerful medicine for colic is ume concentrate

COUGHS, RESPIRATORY ISSUES

Treatment 1: Sunflower Seed (Whole) Tea

· 1 tablespoon sunflower seeds
· 1 cup water

Boil five minutes. Sip a quarter to a half teacupful every two to three hours.

Treatment 2: Mu #16 Tea

Drink at least a half hour before meal.

Treatment 3: Lotus Root Tea

Drink a cup about every three to four hours.

CROOKED SPINE

Treatment: Ginger compress

1. Apply compress. (See Ginger Compress.)

2. Massage firmly for thirty minutes

3. Do this daily for a week. Wait a week, repeat.

DIABETES AND HYPOGLYCEMIA

It is interesting to note that Western doctors have recommended carbohydrates for people suffering from diabetes. This is an ancient Oriental cure. Whole grains are the best-balanced source of carbohydrates. Naturally sweet foods, such as grains, onions, carrots, sweet squash, sweet corn, and jicama, are good for the spleen.

The best food for this condition is adzuki beans cooked with sweet squash (butternut, buttercup, and acorn) and deep-fried scallion roots. Take one rice bowl of adzuki, squash, and two or three scallions root every day for three weeks.

DUODENUNM GASTRIC ULCERS

Fundamental Treatment: Thorough chewing of food; avoidance of soft drinks, fruit juices, and sugary drinks, which interfere with proper chewing and digestion.

If pain occurs two to three hours after meals, the cause is yin. Reduce intake of salt. Excess salt can be a cause of duodenum ulcers.

Symptomatic Treatment: Soy Ginger Plum Bancha Drink. Also, keep a salt plum pit in the mouth for five hours to produce saliva. The salt plum turns to alkaline in the stomach and neutralizes the excess stomach acid that causes ulcers.

EARACHE AND ILLNESS-INDUCED DEAFNESS

Treatment: albi plaster, chlorophyll plaster, or ginger oil may be used externally.

FEVER

Treatment: Barley water made with one part grain to fifteen parts water. Boil twenty minutes, strain and drink six ounces every two to three hours until fever reduces

HEADACHE

This can be considered as primarily a ki disease; a headache always indicates a disturbance in the flow of qi. In women, headache can be a blood disorder occurring at menstruation time. Headache can also represent blood disease in both males and females because of blood stagnation caused by excess animal food. Sharp headache pain is yang, dull pain in yin. Often there is pain only in one part of the head. This usually means that the source of the headache is yang. When the entire head is painful, the cause is generally yin. However, this does not hold true in every case.

External Treatment: Try any of these – tofu plaster or chlorophyll on the forehead; crushed apple and grated radish compress; ginger oil on the head and hair; green leaves on the forehead and back of the neck.

Internal Treatment: Soy bancha is quite effective for yin headaches and migraines

Massage for Headache

Here is a fast way to get rid of a headache or at least to ease the pain. The person should first take light soy bancha drink to improve the circulation. Then massage the shoulder blades. Do not pinch with the fingers but press down with the fleshy part of the thumb. When you have massaged the shoulder blades with the thumbs for three minutes, proceed to pinch lightly with all the fingers. This should not take more than another three minutes.

Next massage the back of the neck. For best results, place yourself at the patient's side, the right hand massaging the neck, and the fingers of the left hand lying on the forehead to control the pressure. Press the head. If this is too painful for the patient, press lightly, increasing the pressure as the patient indicates comfort with the pressure. Massage this area in an orderly manner, line by line, starting from the top and working down. The neck massage can take between three and six minutes. Afterwards, do the back of the head.

Now massage the temples, using much less pressure. Start from the forehead and work to the back of the ear (two minutes). Then press the top of the head, and finish by scratching the entire head with the fingertips – or even with the nails, if necessary – as if you were shampooing the head (one to two minutes).

HICCUPS

Internal Treatment: Steep one teaspoon of dill plant in hot water three to five minutes. Drink as needed.

Tactile Treatment: Apply strong finger pressure on TH #17 (on the jaw line, in line with the bottom of the ear lobe). Firmly press both sides for three to five minutes.

INFLAMED SORE EYE

Treatment: Add 1 spoonful of the pith of a sunflower stalk to a mug of boiling water. Steep for ten minutes. Can be consumed internally as a beverage or externally as a wash.

KIDNEY PROBLEMS

Treatment:

2-3 dried asparagus roots to a mug of boiling water.

Boil for ten to fifteen minutes. Drink one to two cups of this tea a day until changes occur.

Black beans and kidney beans can be used in any form to help the kidneys. See Adzuki Beans preparation.

MORNING SICKNESS, MOTION SICKNESS, SEA SICKNESS

Treatment:

1. Tape an umeboshi seed over the navel.

2. Tape short grain brown rice seed or millet between the two tendons leading into the wrist, about 1 inch above wrist, palm side. (HC #6)

3. Ume concentrate, as needed.

4. Two capsules ginger powder every two to three hours.

PNEUMONIA

Treatment: Avoid meat. When a high fever develops, use albi plaster on forehead and chest. Carp plaster also works nicely. Lotus Root Tea is traditional lung herbal medicine.

RHEUMATISM

This condition may have a possible connection to excessive consumption of sugar or animal protein or mother's excessive consumption of sugar or animal protein during her prenatal and natal history. This condition takes a long period to cure.

Treatment 1: Dilute one teaspoon of miso, preferably Hacho Miso, in small cup of hot water, mix well. Drink slowly, in sips, twice a day

Treatment 2:

· 2-3 tablespoons grated radish
· 1 tablespoon heated sesame oil

· 1 teaspoon soya sauce
  Mix and drink twice a day

May need to reduce liquid intake; excess fluid feeds inflammation. Avoid sugars, sweeteners, dairy products and animal.

Refer to Arthritis Type Symptoms.

SINUS ISSUES (Chronic)

This condition comes from oketsu, "dirty blood," need to clean up your diet.

Treatment: Albi plaster on sinuses. Kuzu-Ginger tea may help.

SKIN ISSUES

Moxa tea is an excellent skin wash. It has anti-bacterial and anti-fungal properties.

Many skin issues, such as eczema, psoriasis, fungal infections, and rashes, are caused by kidney energy/large intestine energy imbalances; often instigated by excessive meat consumption.

The kidneys become overloaded with waste material and the large intestine and skin are forced to share the burden of elimination.

Sugar stimulates and hastens discharge of excess protein and that leads to skin eruptions. Kidney damage from excess protein is the problem; sugar is just the catalyst.

Treatment: Watermelon cleanses the kidneys. Cut out animal fat and protein. Milk is animal fat and protein. Non-fat milk is animal protein.

Symptomatic treatment of kidney issues: Albi plaster on kidney area.

SKIN CARE TREATMENT

Take: fifty percent albi, powdered, + fifty percent French Green Clay, fine powder.

Add: Apple Cider Vinegar* – enough to make a thick paste.

Place in a cheese cloth "mask" for the face.

Apply anywhere using cheese cloth or gauze to secure in place.

Allow to dry. Can leave on for up to eight hours.

Finish with oil rub: Avocado, Olive, or Sesame, or all three.

*Can also try tomato juice or grape juice.

MrTLC

Herbal Skin Immersion Therapy

Mix equal parts of mint, rosemary, thyme, lavender, and comfrey and place in a muslin sachet bag (a small porous bag). Place herbal sachet in an appropriate container, add twenty-four ounces (one and a half pints to three cups) of boiling water and let steep for thirty minutes. Add to bath water. Immerse. Enjoy.

SORE THROAT

Inflammation coming from ineffective or overburdened kidney energy; probably coming from excess consumption of animal protein, salt or liquids.

Internal Treatment: ginger-kuzu tea

External Treatment: Ginger compress or albi plaster

Throat treatment: gargle with strong brew of mugwort (artemisia vulgaris)

STOMACH PAIN AND CRAMPS

There are various ways of taking care of a stomach cramp. To use a pressure point to stop the cramp, push many times with the thumb (maintaining the pressure while you count to three) at the bottom angle of the left shoulder blade. The patient must lie on the stomach, relaxed, arms alongside the body.

External Treatment: ginger compress on stomach.

Internal Treatment: Drink soy ginger salt plum bancha.

If this does not work, supplement with ten to twenty powdered fennel seeds powdered; add to any tea or sprinkle on foods.

The ideal treatment is a balanced diet, which builds the nervous system. The nervous system needs vitamin B. The best natural supply of this vitamin is whole grains.

TONSILITIS

Tonsilitis is a sign the patient needs to strengthen the immune system.

Internal Treatment: kuzu-ginger tea (can add cinnamon, dates, licorice root, and peony root)

External Treastment: albi plaster

In addition, you may try the following

1. Sage – Simmer a handful of herb in fat or vegetable oil. Take two teaspoons, four to five times daily.

2. Moxa – Infuse a pinch of herb in four to six ounces of water for three to five minutes. Use as a gargle every hour.

TOOTHACHE

Treatment: Pinch and firmly rub the triangular area on the back of the hand, between the thumb and index finger.

Apply Dentie to aching tooth. Dentie is a dental powder made of carbonized eggplant and sea salt. It is available from macrobiotic stores and via the Internet. I use www.goldminenaturalfoods.com

WOUNDS

For lacerations, incisions, avulsions, any cuts to the flesh, use moxa to stop the bleeding, fight infection, and decrease scarring.

Take a pinch of moxa, enough to cover the wound. Lightly dampen (traditionally, the injured person chews the moxa), place on wound and bandage. Change the moxa every few hours and keep it on until the wound begins to heal.

Moxa tea is an excellent skin wash. It has anti-bacteria and anti-fungal properties.

FINALLY

From the Columbia Cook Book (1892) by Mrs. H.E.
Hollingsworth, published by C.R. Parish & Co.,
Philadelphia/Toronto

> "It is plainly seen by an inquiring mind that,
> aside from the selection and preparation of food,
> there are many little things constantly arising in
> the experience of everyday life which, in their
> combined effect, are powerful agents in the
> formation (or prevention) of perfect health. A
> careful observance of these little occurrences,
> an inquiry into the philosophy attending to them
> lies within the province, and indeed should be
> considered among the highest duties of every
> housekeeper human." (Yes, my alteration)

"True worth is in being, not seeming.

In doing each day that goes by,

Some little good – not in dreaming

Of great things to do by and by."

Alice Cary

"Know then, thyself,

Presume not God to scan.

The proper study of mankind is man."

Alexander Pope

AND REALLY

A fifth-grade pupil in Seattle gave this description in a homework paper:

"The human body is composed of three parts – the branium, the borax, and the abominable cavity. The branium contains the brain. The borax contains the lungs, the liver and living things. The abominable cavity contains the bowels, of which there are five: A, E, I, O, U."

I wish you all knowledge, wisdom, smiles, hugs.

What you can use, use, add to it, pass it on.

It really is all about us.

Thomas Duckworth, Spring 2017

Made in United States
Orlando, FL
02 November 2021

10171737R00059